CHRIST ON THE CROSS, WITH THE VIRGIN AND ST. JOHN.
Austrian, c. 1410. Wood; h. 33½, w. 31⅞ ins. (85 x 81 cm.). Acquired in
St. Petersburg, 1908.

MASTERPIECES
from the
BERLIN MUSEUMS

EXHIBITED IN COOPERATION
WITH THE DEPARTMENT OF
THE ARMY OF THE UNITED
STATES OF AMERICA

1948-1949

AT

THE DETROIT INSTITUTE OF ARTS

THE CLEVELAND MUSEUM OF ART

THE MINNEAPOLIS INSTITUTE OF ARTS

THE M. H. DE YOUNG MEMORIAL MUSEUM, SAN FRANCISCO

THE LOS ANGELES COUNTY MUSEUM

THE CITY ART MUSEUM OF ST. LOUIS

CARNEGIE INSTITUTE, PITTSBURGH

THE TOLEDO MUSEUM OF ART

PRINTED BY THE ARTCRAFT PRINTING COMPANY
CLEVELAND

COPYRIGHT, 1948
THE CLEVELAND MUSEUM OF ART

INTRODUCTION

AMERICAN armies advancing through Germany in the spring of 1945 discovered in a salt mine at Merkers a cache of important pictures from the Berlin museums. Although the cache represented only a small portion of the collection of the Kaiser-Friedrich-Museum, Berlin, it included some of the world's great masterpieces and the group may be said to represent the cream of one of the world's great collections of the old masters. Also included in the cache were two master-pieces from the National-Galerie, Berlin, the museum devoted to the art of the nineteenth and twentieth centuries.

This group of paintings was brought to the United States for safekeeping on the Army transport *James Parker* in December, 1945, and deposited by the Department of the Army in the vaults of the National Gallery of Art in Washington, D. C.

In the spring of 1948 General Lucius D. Clay, United States Military Governor of Germany, reported that safe storage facilities had been made available in the American zone of occupation and that the paintings could be returned to Germany to be held there in the custody of American authorities pending the final peace settlement.

By a decision of the Department of the Army, the paintings which, because of age and fragility could not be subjected to the risks of further travel, were returned in the spring of 1948 to Germany; but the remainder were made available, under the supervision of the Army, for exhibition in a certain number of American museums in the principal regions of the country, the proceeds from the exhibition to go to the German Children's Relief Fund administered by the American authorities in Germany.

This in brief is the history of the remarkable group of pictures represented in this book. The two pictures from the National-Galerie are *Don Quixote* by Honoré Daumier and *The Green-house* by Édouard Manet; all the remainder are from the collection of the Kaiser-Friedrich-Museum.

CATALOGUE

All the paintings in the exhibition come from the Kaiser-Friedrich-Museum, Berlin, except those by Daumier and Manet, which come from the National-Galerie, Berlin. The information for the captions was taken from recent catalogues of these museums. Sizes in inches have been added.

AUSTRIAN

THE LAMENTATION OVER CHRIST. Austrian, c. 1425. Wood; h. 9⅞, w. 10¼ ins. (25 × 24 cm.). Acquired in Berlin, 1918.

DUTCH

IRGIN AND CHILD. Geertgen tot Sint Jans, Dutch, c. 1465-c. 1493. Wood; h. 31⅞, w. 20½
s. (81 x 52 cm.). Painted in ripe period of master. Acquired from von Hollitscher, 1919.

PORTRAIT OF A MAN. Jan Mostaert, Dutch, c. 1475-1555/56. Wood; h. 16½, w. 11⅜ ins. (42 x 29 cm.). Acquired from Royal Collections, Berlin and Potsdam, 1829.

THE ADORATION OF THE MAGI. The Master of the Virgin among Virgins,
Dutch, act. 1460-70 to 1495. Wood; h. 24¾, w. 18⅞ ins. (63 x 48 cm.). Gift of
Jacques Seligmann, Paris, 1910.

MALLE BABBE, THE WITCH OF HAARLEM. Frans Hals, Dutch, 1585-1666.
Another version is in The Metropolitan Museum of Art. Canvas; h. 29½, w. 25³⁄₁₆ ins.
(75 x 64 cm.). Painted in later period of master. Acquired from Suermondt, 1874.

SINGING BOY WITH A FLUTE. Frans Hals, Dutch, 1585-1666. Canvas;
h. 25⅝, w. 21¼ ins. (65 x 54 cm.). Painted c. 1625. Signed lower right: F H
(monogram). Acquired from Suermondt, 1874.

PORTRAIT OF A YOUNG MAN. Frans Hals, Dutch, 1585-1666. Canvas;
h. 29½, w. 22⅞ ins. (75 x 58 cm.). Acquired 1840.

PORTRAIT OF A YOUNG WOMAN. Frans Hals, Dutch, 1585-1666.
Canvas; h. 29½, w. 22⅞ ins. (75 x 58 cm.). Painted c. 1630. Acquired 1841.

PORTRAIT OF TYMAN OOSDORP (died 1668). Frans Hals, Dutch,
1585-1666. Canvas; h. 31½, w. 27½ ins. (80 x 70 cm.). Acquired 1877.

A LITTLE GIRL WITH HER NURSE. Frans Hals, Dutch, 1585-1666.
Canvas; h. 33⅞, w. 25⅝ ins. (86 x 65 cm.). Acquired from Suermondt, 1874.

THE PREACHING OF ST. JOHN THE BAPTIST. Rembrandt, Dutch, 1606-1669. Canvas on wood;

DANIEL'S VISION. Rembrandt, Dutch, 1606-1669. Canvas; h. 37¾, w. 45⅝ ins. (96 x 116 cm.). Painted c. 1650. Acquired in Paris, 1883.

PORTRAIT OF A RABBI. Rembrandt, Dutch, 1606-1669. Canvas; h. 43¼, w. 32¼ ins. (110 x 82 cm.). Signed lower left: REMBRANDT./F. 1645. Acquired from Suermondt, 1874.

THE MAN WITH THE GOLDEN HELMET. Rembrandt, Dutch, 1606-
1669. Rembrandt's brother Adriaen (1597/98-1654). Canvas: h. 26⅜,
w. 19¾ ins. (67 x 50 cm.). Painted c. 1650. Acquired in London by the
Kaiser-Friedrich-Museums-Verein, 1897.

TOBIAS AND THE ANGEL. Rembrandt, Dutch, 1606-1669. Canvas;
h. 33⅞, w. 29⅛ ins. (86 x 74 cm.). Painted c. 1650. Signed later, lower
left: R. . . Gift of Wilhelm von Bode, 1910.

OLD MAN WITH A RED CAP. Rembrandt, Dutch, 1606-1669. Canvas; h. 20, w. 14⁹⁄₁₆ ins. (51 x 37 cm.). Painted c. 1655. Acquired in London, 1890.

JOSEPH AND POTIPHAR'S WIFE. Rembrandt, Dutch, 1606-1669. Canvas; h. 43¼, w. 34¼ ins. (110 x 87 cm.). Signed on Joseph's coat, lower right: REMBRAN/F: 1655. Acquired in Paris, 1883.

MOSES BREAKING THE TABLETS OF THE LAW. Rembrandt, Dutch,
1606-1669. Scholars have recently suggested that the subject represents
Moses showing the tablets. Canvas; h. 65¾, w. 53⅛ ins. (167 x 135 cm.).
Signed lower right: REMBRANDT F. 1659. Acquired from Royal Collections,
Berlin and Potsdam, 1829.

PORTRAIT OF HENDRICKJE STOFFELS. Rembrandt, Dutch, 1606-1669. Canvas; h. 33⅞, w. 25⅝ ins. (86 x 65 cm.). Painted c. 1658/59. Acquired in Paris, 1879.

HAARLEM FROM DUNES AT OVERVEEN. Jacob van Ruisdael, Dutch, 1628/29-1682. Canvas; h. 20½, w. 25⅝ ins. (52 x 65 cm.). Signed lower right: JVRUISDAEL. Painted c. 1670. Acquired from Suermondt, 1874.

VIEW OF RHENEN. Hercules Seghers, Dutch, c. 1589–c. 1645. Wood; h. 16½, w. 26 ins. (42 x 66 cm.).
Signed lower left: HERCULES SEGERS. Acquired from Suermondt, 1874.

PANORAMA OF HOLLAND. Philips Koninck, Dutch, 1619-1688. Canvas; h. 35⅞, w. 65 ins. (91 x 165 cm.).
Signed lower right: P. KONING. Acquired in London, 1888.

STILL LIFE. Willem Kalf, Dutch, 1621/22-1693. Cavas; h. 25³⁄₁₆, w. 20⅞ ins. (64 x 53 cm.). Acquired in Paris, 1899.

STILL LIFE. Willem Kalf, Dutch, 1621/22-1693. Canvas; h. 25⅝, w. 22 ins.
(65 x 56 cm.). Gift of Sir Julius Wernher, London, 1893.

THE MOTHER. Pieter de Hooch, Dutch, 1629-c. 1683. Canvas; h. 36¼,
w. 39⅜ ins. (92 x 100 cm.). Painted c. 1659/60. Acquired from Schneider,
Paris, 1876.

THE BUGLER. Pieter de Hooch, Dutch, 1629-c. 1683. Canvas; h. 33½, w. 36⅝ ins. (85 x 93 cm.). Painted c. 1671-74. Acquired in Paris, 1867.

THE GARDEN OF THE INN. Jan Steen, Dutch, c. 1626-1679. Canvas; h. 26¾, w. 22⅞ ins. (68 x 58 cm.). Signed on stretcher of table: JSTEEN. Acquired from Royal Collections, Berlin and Potsdam, 1829.

BAPTISMAL PARTY. Jan Steen, Dutch, c. 1626-1679. Canvas; h. 32⅝, w. 39 ins. (83 x 99 cm.).
Signed lower left: JSTEEN. Inscribed on paper in foreground: SO DE OUDE SONGEN/SO PYPEN DE JONGEN.
Acquired from Lord Francis Pelham Clinton Hope, London, 1901.

37

FATHERLY ADVICE. Gerard Terborch, Dutch, 1617-1681. Canvas;
h. 27½, w. 23⅝ ins. (70 x 60 cm.). Acquired from Giustiniani before 1815.

YOUNG LADY WITH A PEARL NECKLACE. Jan Vermeer, Dutch, 1632–
1675. Canvas; h. 21⅝, w. 17¾ ins. (55 x 45 cm.). Signed on side of table top:
JVMEER. Painted in late period of master. Acquired from Suermondt, 1874.

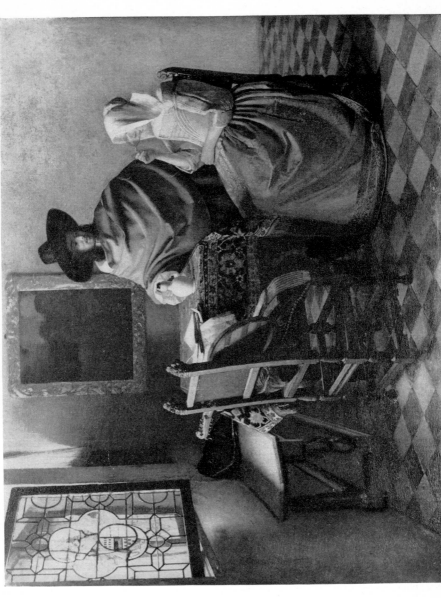

LADY AND GENTLEMAN DRINKING WINE. Jan Vermeer, Dutch, 1632-1675. Canvas; h. 25⅝, w. 30¼ in. (65 x 77 cm.). Acquired from Lord Francis Pelham Clinton Hope London, 1901.

THE FARM. Adriaen van de Velde, Dutch, c. 1636-1672. Canvas on wood; h. 24¾, w. 30¾ ins. (63 x 78 cm.). Signed on fence, left: A. V. VELDE. F/1666. Acquired fr. Lord Francis Pelham Clinton Hope, London, 1899.

A ROAD WINDING AMONGST CLUMPS OF TREES AND SMALL FARMS. Meindert Hobbema,

Panel 96.5 × 129.5 cm. Painted c. 1665. Acquired 1926

FLEMISH

THE VIRGIN AND CHILD. Hans Memling, Flemish, c. 1433-1494.Wood;
h. 16⅞, w. 12¼ ins. (43 x 31 cm.). Painted c. 1487. Acquired 1862.

THE VIRGIN AND CHILD ENTHRONED WITH AN ANGEL. Hans
Memling, Flemish, c. 1433-1494. Wood; h. 26, w. 18¼ ins. (66 x 46.5 cm.).
Gift of Adolf Thiem, San Remo, 1904.

(a, b, c) JOYS AND SORROWS OF MARY. Workshop of Rogier van der Weyden, Flemish, XV Century. Critics believe this triptych, formerly in Convent of Miraflores, near Burgos, Spain, to be a fine 15th-century copy of similar altarpiece by Rogier van der Weyden. (a, b, c) Wood; h. 27⅞, w. 16⅞ ins. (71 x 43 cm.). Acquired from King William II of Holland, The Hague, 1850.

THE REST ON THE FLIGHT INTO EGYPT. Joachim Patinir, Flemish, c. 1485-1524. Wood; h. 24⅜, w. 30¾ ins. (62 x 78 cm.). Acquired from Edward Solly, London, 1821.

47

THE MOURNING MAGDALEN. Quentin Massys, Flemish, 1465/66-1530.
Wood; h. 13, w. 9½ ins. (33 x 24 cm.). Painted in ripe period of master.
Acquired by exchange, 1896.

PORTRAIT OF A YOUNG MAN WITH A GLOVE. Joos van Cleve,
Flemish, act. by 1507; died 1540/41. Wood; h. 24⅜, w. 18½ ins. (62 x 47 cm.).
Painted in late period of master. Acquired from Reimer, Berlin, 1843.

THE VIRGIN AND CHILD ENTHRONED WITH SAINTS. Peter Paul
Rubens, Flemish, 1577-1640. Wood; h. 31⅛, w. 215⅝ ins. (79 x 55 cm.). Acquired from Royal Collections, Berlin and Potsdam, 1829.

FRENCH

ÉTIENNE CHEVALIER AND ST. STEPHEN. Jean Fouquet, French,
1415-20 to 1477-81. Wood; h. 36⅝, w. 33½ ins. (93 x 85 cm.). Inscribed at left:
[CHEVAL]IER ESTIEN[NE]. Acquired from Brentano, Frankfurt-am-Main, 1896.

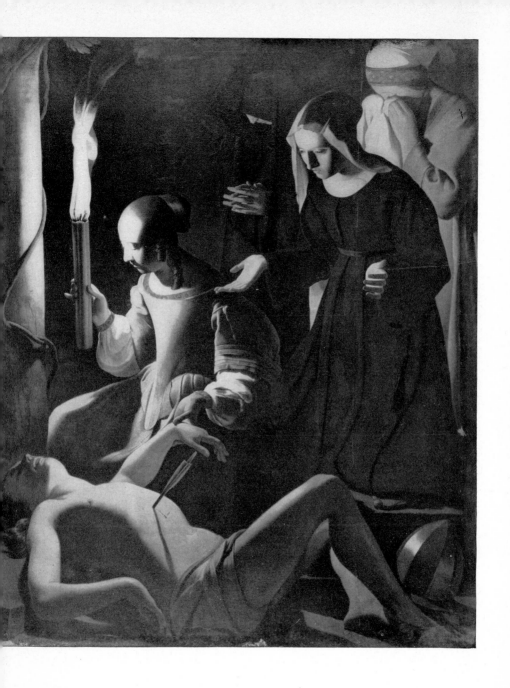

ST. SEBASTIAN MOURNED BY ST. IRENE AND HER LADIES.
Georges de La Tour, French, 1600-1652. Canvas; h. 63, w. 50¾ ins. (160 x
129 cm.). Gift of the Matthiessen Gallery, Berlin, 1928.

LANDSCAPE WITH SAINT MATTHEW AND THE ANGEL. Nicolas Poussin, French, 1593/94-1665.

JUPITER NOURISHED BY THE GOAT AMALTHEA. Nicolas Poussin, French, 1593/94-1665. Canvas; h. 38¼, w. 52⅜ ins. (97 x 133 cm.). Painted in middle period of master. Acquired from Royal Collections, Berlin and Potsdam, 1829.

ITALIAN LANDSCAPE. Claude Lorrain (Gellée), French, c. 1600-1682. Liber Veritatis, no. 64. Canvas: h. 38¼, w.

THE FRENCH COMEDIANS. Antoine Watteau, French, 1684-1721. Canvas; h. 14⁹⁄₁₆, w. 18⅞ ins. (37 x 48 cm.). Acquired from Royal Collections, Berlin and Potsdam, 1829.

THE ITALIAN COMEDIANS. Antoine Watteau, French, 1684-1721. Canvas; h. 14⁹⁄₁₆,

OUTDOOR FESTIVAL. Antoine Watteau, French, 1684-1721. Canvas; h. 43¾, w. 64¼ ins. (111 x 163 cm.). Not finished. Acquired from Royal Collections, Berlin and Potsdam, 1889.

THE DRAFTSMAN. Jean-Baptiste-Siméon Chardin, French, 1699-1779. Canvas; h. 31⅞, w. 25³⁄₁₆ ins. (81 x 64 cm.). Signed and dated left center: CHARDIN/1737. Acquired 1931.

STILL LIFE WITH PHEASANT. Jean-Baptiste-Siméon Chardin, French,
1699-1779. Canvas; h. 29⅛, w. 23⅝ ins. (74 x 60 cm.). Signed and dated right
center: CHARDIN. F./1760. Gift of Thomas Agnew and Sons, London, 1925.

DON QUIXOTE AND SANCHO PANZA. Honoré Daumier, French, 1808-1879. Canvas; h. 30¾, w. 47¼ ins. (78 x 120 cm.). Signed lower right: h. b. National-Galerie, Berlin. Gift of Alfred Beit, London, 1906. (Removed from exhibition.)

THE GREENHOUSE. Edouard Manet, French, 1832-1883. M. and Mme. Guillemet, friends of the artist. Canvas; h. 45¼, w. 59 ins. (115 x 150 cm.). Signed and dated lower left: MANET 1879. National-Galerie, Berlin. Gift of Berlin Friends of Art, 1896.

GERMAN

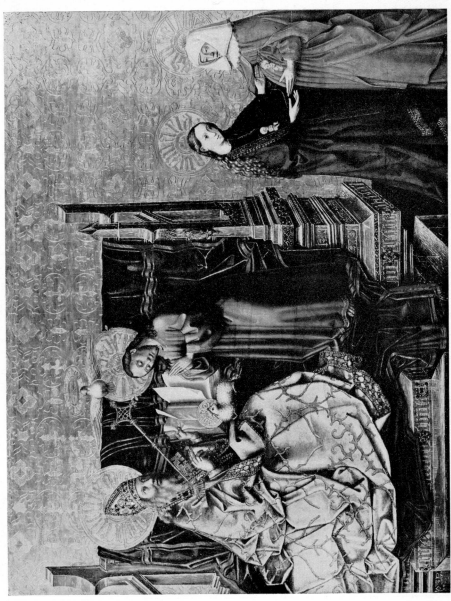

THE DECISION ON THE REDEMPTION OF MAN. Konrat Witz, German, c. 1398-1447. From St. Peter

THE NATIVITY. Martin Schongauer, German, c. 1445-1491. Probably originally the center of a small altarpiece. Wood; h. 14¾, w. 11 ins. (37.5 x 28 cm.). Painted in middle period of master. Acquired in London by the Kaiser-Friedrich-Museums-Verein, 1902.

THE VIRGIN IN PRAYER. Albrecht Dürer, German, 1471-1528. Wood; h. 20⅞, w. 16⅞ ins. (53 x 43 cm.). Signed and dated upper left: 1518/AD (monogram). Gift of Wilhelm von Bode, 1894.

PORTRAIT OF THE WIFE OF JOHANN REUSS. Lucas Cranach the
Elder, German, 1472-1553. Wood; h. 20½, w. 14³⁄₁₆ ins. (52 x 36 cm.).
Acquired in Berlin, 1923.

LUCRETIA. Lucas Cranach the Elder, German, 1472-1553. Wood; h. 14, w. 8½ ins. (35.5 x 21.5 cm.). Signed and dated lower left: 1533/ (winged serpent). Bequest of Ludwig Knauss heirs, 1917.

THE HOLY FAMILY. Hans Burgkmair, German, 1473-1531. Wood; h. 28¾, w. 20⅞ ins. (73 x 53 cm.). Painted c. 1525. Acquired in Cassel, 1915.

COUNT VON LÖWENSTEIN. Hans Baldung (Grün), German, 1475-80 to 1545. Wood; h. 18⅛, w. 13 ins. (46 x 33 cm.). Inscribed above. Signed and dated: .HB (monogram) /1513. Acquired by the Kaiser-Friedrich-Museums-Verein, 1918.

THE NATIVITY. Albrecht Altdorfer, German, c. 1480-1538. Wood; h. 14³⁄₁₆, w. 10 ins. (36 x 25.5 cm.). Painted c. 1513. Acquired from Charles Butler, London, 1892.

NOAH'S THANK OFFERING. Adam Elsheimer (?), German, 1578-1610.

ST. CHRISTOPHER. Adam Elsheimer (?), German, 1578-1610. Copper; h. 8¼, w. 11 ins. (21 x 28 cm.). Acquired by gift, 1913.

PORTRAIT OF THE COSMOGRAPHER SEBASTIAN MÜNSTER
(1489-1552). Christoph Amberger, German, c. 1500-1561/62. Wood; h. 21¼,
w. 16½ ins. (54 x 42 cm.). Acquired before 1820.

ITALIAN

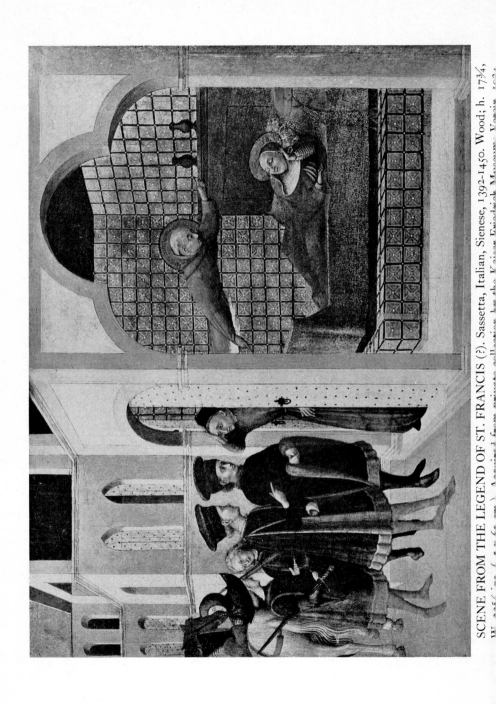

SCENE FROM THE LEGEND OF ST. FRANCIS (?). Sassetta, Italian, Sienese, 1392-1450. Wood; h. 17¾,
W. 12¼ in. (45 x 62 cm.). Acquired from private collection by the Kaiser Friedrich Museum, Venice, 1931.

THE CRUCIFIXION. Giovanni di Paolo, Italian, Sienese, 1402/03-1482. Tempera, wood; h. 12⅝, w. 9 1/16 ins. (32 x 23 cm.). Acquired from Edward Solly, London, 1821.

THE RESURRECTION OF CHRIST. Giovanni Bellini, Italian, Venetian,
c. 1430-1516. Wood; h. 58¼, w. 50⅜ ins. (148 x 128 cm.). Acquired in Italy, 1903.

← (a) THE CLOTHING OF ST. CLARE BY ST. FRANCIS. (b) ST. CLARE
SAVING A SHIP IN DISTRESS. (a, b) Giovanni di Paolo, Italian, Sienese,
1402/03-1482. (a) Wood; h. 7⅞, w. 11⅜ ins. (20 x 29 cm.). (b) Wood; h. 7¾,
w. 11½ ins. (19.5 x 29.4 cm.). (a, b) Acquired fr. Harry Fuld, Frankfurt-am-Main.

THE BURIAL OF CHRIST. Vittore Carpaccio, Italian, Venetian, c. 1455-1525/26. Canvas; h. 57⅛, w. 72⅞ ins. (145 x 185 cm.). Painted in late period of master. Signed falsely on base of table: ANDREAS MANTINEA. F. Acquired

LEDA AND THE SWAN. Correggio, Italian, Parmesan, c. 1494-1534. Canvas; h. 59⅞, w. 75¼ ins. (152 x 191 cm.). Painted c. 1530. Acquired from Royal Collections, Berlin and Potsdam, 1829.

ALLEGORY OF MUSIC. Filippino Lippi, Italian, Florentine, c. 1457-1504. Tempera, wood; h. 24, w. 20 ins. (61 x 51 cm.). Painted in late period of master. Acquired from Landsinger, Florence, 1883.

← VENUS. Sandro Botticelli, Italian, Florentine, 1444/45-1510. Tempera, canvas; h. 61⅞, w. 26¾ ins. (157 x 68 cm.). Painted c. 1478. Acquired from Edward Solly, London, 1821.

PORTRAIT OF A YOUNG MAN. Sebastiano Mainardi, Italian, Florentine, c. 1460-1513. Tempera, wood; h. 16⅞, w. 13 ins. (43 x 33 cm.). Acquired through Baron von Rumohr, 1829.

PORTRAIT OF A YOUNG LADY. Lorenzo di Credi (?), Italian, Florentine, c. 1459-1537. Wood; h. 17¾, w. 11⅜ ins. (45 x 29 cm.). Inscribed below: NOLI ME TANGERE. Acquired through Baron von Rumohr, 1829.

PORTRAIT OF A YOUNG MAN. Agnolo Bronzino, Italian, Florentine, 1503-1572. Wood; h. 33⅞, w. 26⅜ ins. (85 x 67 cm.). Acquired from Edward Solly, London, 1821.

PORTRAIT OF A YOUTH. Agnolo Bronzino, Italian, Florentine, 1503-1572.
Wood; h. 22⅞, w. 18½ ins. (58 x 47 cm.). Acquired in Florence.

CHRIST TAKING LEAVE OF HIS MOTHER. Lorenzo Lotto, Italian, Venetian, c. 1480-1556. The picture was painted for Domenico Tassi of Bergamo, whose wife appears in the right foreground. Canvas; h. 49⅝, w. 39 ins. (126 x 99 cm.). Signed on letter, lower center: A°LAURENTJO/LOTTO PICTOR/1521. Acquired from Edward Solly, London, 1821.

PORTRAIT OF A YOUNG MAN. Titian, Italian, Venetian, c. 1477-1576.
Drawn by Van Dyck in his Italian Sketchbook. Canvas: h. 37, w. 28⅜ ins.
(94 x 72 cm.). Painted c. 1525. Signed left center: TIZIANUS/.F. Acquired from
Royal Collections, Berlin and Potsdam, 1829.

PORTRAIT OF A DAUGHTER OF ROBERTO STROZZI. Titian, Italian,
Venetian, c. 1477-1576. Canvas; h. 45¼, w. 38⅝ ins. (115 x 98 cm.). Signed
on the side of pedestal top: TITIANVS F. Inscribed upper left: ANNOR' II.
MDXLII. Acquired from Palazzo Strozzi, Florence, 1878.

TITIAN'S DAUGHTER LAVINIA. Titian, Italian, Venetian, c. 1477-1576.
Canvas; h. 40⅛, w. 32¼ ins. (102 x 82 cm.). Painted c. 1550, perhaps for
Nicolò Grasso. Acquired from Abbot Celotti, Florence, 1832.

SELF-PORTRAIT. Titian, Italian, Venetian, c. 1477-1576. Canvas; h. 37¾,
w. 29½ ins. (96 x 75 cm.). Not finished. Acquired from Edward Solly, London, 1821.

VENUS WITH THE ORGAN PLAYER. Titian, Italian, Venetian, c. 1477-1576. Canvas; h. 45¼, w. 82¾ ins. (115 x 210 cm.). Signed lower left: TITIANVS. F. Acquired in Vienna with the help of patrons of the Kaiser-Friedrich-Museum, 1918.

PORTRAIT OF A MAN WITH A WHITE BEARD. Tintoretto, Italian,
Venetian, 1518-1594. Canvas; h. 22⅞, w. 17¼ ins. (58 x 44 cm.). Painted in
late period of master. Acquired in England, 1908.

PORTRAIT OF DOGE MOCENIGO. Tintoretto, Italian, Venetian, 1518-
1594. Canvas; h. 43½, w. 38 ins. (110.5 x 96.5 cm.).

PORTRAIT OF A KNIGHT OF ST. JAMES. Sebastiano del Piombo (?),
Italian, Venetian, c. 1485-1547. Canvas; h. 43¾, w. 35⅞ ins. (111 x 91 cm.).
Acquired from Marchese Patrizi, Rome, 1875.

JUDITH WITH THE HEAD OF HOLOFERNES. Bernardo Strozzi,
Italian, Genoese, 1581-1644. Canvas; h. 48⅞, w. 37 ins. (124 x 94 cm.).
Acquired in Rome by the Kaiser-Friedrich-Museums-Verein, 1914.

ALESSANDRO DEL BORRO (?). Andrea Sacchi (?), Italian, Roman, 1599-1661. Canvas; h. 79⅞, w. 47⅝ ins. (203 x 121 cm.). Acquired in Florence, 1873.

LOVE AS CONQUEROR. Michelangelo da Caravaggio, Italian, Roman, c. 1573-c. 1610.
Canvas; h. 60⅝, w. 43¼ ins. (154 x 110 cm.). Painted c. 1600. Acquired fr. Giustiniani, 1815.

TWO PHYSICIANS AS SS. COSMAS AND DAMIAN. Giovanni Battista Caracciolo, Italian, Neapolitan, 1570–1637.

ROMAN LANDSCAPE. Giovanni Paolo Panini, Italian, Roman, 1691/92-1765. Canvas; h. 38⅝, w. 52¾ ins. (98 x 134 cm.). Signed on stone, lower left: P. PANINI/ ROMA/ 1735. Acquired in London, 1882.

RINALDO IN ARMIDA'S ENCHANTED GARDEN. Giovanni Battista Tiepolo, Italian, Venetian, 1696-1770. Sketch for the picture painted 1751-53 for the Würzburger Residenz. Canvas; h. 15⅜, w. 24⅜ ins. (39 x 62 cm.). Acquired in England, 1908.

CHRIST BEARING THE CROSS. Giovanni Battista Tiepolo, Italian, Venetian, 1696-1770. Sketch for the painting done in 1749 for Sant' Alvise, Venice. Canvas; h. 20½, w. 24¾ ins. (52 x 63 cm.). Acquired 1906.

THE MARTYRDOM OF ST. AGATHA. Tiepolo, Italian, Venetian, 1696-1770. Picture painted c. 1756 for the Church of Sant' Agata in Lendinara. Canvas; h. 72⅜, w. 51½ ins. (184 x 131 cm.). Acquired in Paris, 1878.

A BALLOON ASCENSION OVER THE GIUDECCA, VENICE. Francesco
Guardi, Italian, Venetian, 1712-1793. Canvas; h. 26, w. 20 ins. (66 x 51 cm.).
Acquired by the Kaiser-Friedrich-Museums-Verein, 1901.

PIAZZA SAN MARCO, VENICE. Francesco Guardi, Italian, Venetian, 1712–1793. Canvas; h. 21½, w. 26 ins. (54.5 x 66 cm.). Acquired by the Kaiser-Friedrich-Museums-Verein, 1906.

THE PIAZZETTA, VENICE. Francesco Guardi, Italian, Venetian, 1712-1793. Canvas; h. 11¼, w. 17¼ ins. (28.5 x 44 cm.). Gift of Wilhelm von Bode, 1918.

PORTRAIT OF A LADY AS DIANA. Jacopo Amigoni, Italian, Venetian,
1675-1752. Canvas; h. 50⅜, w. 37 ins. (128 x 94 cm.). Gift of Franz von
Mendelssohn, 1908.

SPANISH

PORTRAIT OF THE COUNTESS OLIVARES. Velázquez, Spanish, 1599-1660. Canvas; h. 47¼, w. 39 ins. (120 x 99 cm.). Painted c. 1631-33. Acquired from Earl of Dudley, London, 1887.

INDEX

CHANGES IN THE EXHIBITION SINCE PUBLICATION
OF THE CATALOGUE

At a meeting in Boston on August 30, the Committee for the Department of the Army withdrew 14 pictures from the exhibition, as a precaution against damage. At the same time the Department of the Army authorized the inclusion of the following 12 pictures:

10. BOTTICELLI	. . . . .	Portrait of Simonetta Vespucci
14. BOUTS, DIERIC	. . . . .	The Virgin in Adoration
15. BOUTS, DIERIC	. . . . .	The Virgin and Child
19. BRUEGEL, PIETER, the ELDER	. . .	Two Fettered Apes
37. DOMENICO VENEZIANO	. . .	The Martyrdom of St. Lucy
47. GIORGIONE	. . . . .	Portrait of a Young Man
51. JAN GOSSART (MABUSE)	. . . .	Portrait of a Man
62. HOLBEIN	. . . .	Portrait of an Elderly Man
70. VAN LEYDEN		The Chess Players
93. REMBRANDT	. . . . .	Self-Portrait
96. REMBRANDT	. . . . .	Susanna and the Elders
105. RUBENS	. . . .	Landscape with the Shipwreck of Aeneas

KEY TO NUMBERS ON PICTURE LABELS

2. p. 73, withdrawn	**52.** p. 107	**98.** p. 21
4. p. 76	**53.** p. 109	**99.** p. 24
5. p. 110	**54.** p. 108	**100.** p. 26
6. p. 2	**55.** p. 16	**101.** p. 25
7. p. 8	**56.** p. 17	**102.** p. 28
8. p. 72	**57.** p. 15	**103.** p. 27, withdrawn
9. p. 81, withdrawn	**58.** p. 18	**105.** Not in catalogue
10. Not in catalogue	**59.** p. 14	**106.** p. 50
13. p. 84	**60.** p. 19	**109.** p. 29
14. Not in catalogue	**61.** p. 42	**110.** p. 100
15. Not in catalogue	**62.** Not in catalogue	**111.** p. 78
16. p. 89	**63.** p. 34	**113.** p. 67, withdrawn
18. p. 88	**64.** p. 35	**115.** p. 98
19. Not in catalogue	**65.** p. 49	**116.** p. 30
20. p. 71	**66.** p. 32, withdrawn	**119.** p. 37
22. p. 102	**67.** p. 33	**120.** p. 36
23. p. 101, withdrawn	**68.** p. 31	**121.** p. 99
24. p. 82, withdrawn	**69.** p. 53, withdrawn	**123.** p. 38
26. p. 60	**70.** Not in catalogue	**124.** p. 105
27. p. 61	**71.** p. 85	**125.** p. 104
28. p. 56	**72.** p. 90	**126.** p. 106
30. p. 83	**73.** p. 86	**127.** p. 97
32. p. 69	**74.** p. 63	**128.** p. 96
34. p. 70	**78.** p. 48	**129.** p. 91
35. p. 87	**79.** p. 13	**130.** p. 92
36. p. 62, withdrawn	**80.** p. 44	**131.** p. 93
37. Not in catalogue	**82.** p. 45	**132.** p. 95
38. p. 68, withdrawn	**84.** p. 12	**133.** p. 94
41. p. 74	**86.** p. 103, withdrawn	**136.** p. 113
42. p. 75	**87.** p. 47	**137.** p. 41
44. p. 52, withdrawn	**88.** p. 54	**138.** p. 39
46. p. 11	**89.** p. 55	**139.** p. 40, withdrawn
47. Not in catalogue	**93.** Not in catalogue	**141.** p. 57
48. p. 79	**94.** p. 20	**142.** p. 58
49.⎫	**95.** p. 22	**143.** p. 59
50.⎭ p. 80, withdrawn	**96.** Not in catalogue	**146.** p. 46
51. Not in catalogue	**97.** p. 23	**147.** p. 66, withdrawn

Th. Kenlon